Rhoda Hershberger from Mom '97

ideals®
THANKSGIVING

More Than 50 Years of Celebrating Life's Most Treasured Moments

Vol. 54, No. 5

"O Lord! that lends me life,
Lend me a heart replete with thankfulness!"

—William Shakespeare

IDEALS—Vol. 54, No. 5 September MCMXCVII IDEALS (ISSN 0019-137X) is published six times a year: January, March, May, July, September, and November by IDEALS PUBLICATIONS INCORPORATED, 535 Metroplex Drive, Suite 250, Nashville, TN 37211.
Periodical postage paid at Nashville, Tennessee, and additional mailing offices.
Copyright © MCMXCVII by IDEALS PUBLICATIONS INCORPORATED.
POSTMASTER: Send address changes to Ideals, PO Box 305300, Nashville, TN 37230. All rights reserved.
Title IDEALS registered U.S. Patent Office.

SINGLE ISSUE—U.S. $5.95 USD; Higher in Canada
ONE-YEAR SUBSCRIPTION—U.S. $19.95 USD; Canada $36.00 CDN (incl. GST and shipping); Foreign $25.95 USD
TWO-YEAR SUBSCRIPTION—U.S. $35.95 USD; Canada $66.50 CDN (incl. GST and shipping); Foreign $47.95 USD

Printed and bound in USA by Quebecor Printing. Printed on Weyerhaeuser Husky.

The paper used in this publication meets the minimum requirements of
American National Standard for Information Sciences—
Permanence of Paper for Printed Library Materials, ANSI Z39.48-1984.

Subscribers may call customer service at 1-800-558-4343 to make address changes.
Unsolicited manuscripts will not be returned without a self-addressed, stamped envelope.

ISBN 0-8249-1145-8 GST 131903775

Cover Photo
HARVEST GIFTS
Larry LeFever/Grant Heilman Photography

Inside Covers
THE 12:09—ON TIME AGAIN!
Jane Wooster Scott, artist
Superstock

Gifts of Fall

Paula Sampson

We thank Thee, Father up above,
    For all Thy autumn gifts of love.
You give us beauty unsurpassed—
    Resplendent scenes of brilliance massed.

And to Thee this we also owe:
    The ample harvests that we know;
But to Thee, Father, most of all,
    We thank Thee for creating fall.

Autumn's Song

Becky Jennings

When prairie fields are tinted brown
    And purple grapes hang low,
Then pungent odors fill the town
    Where autumn bonfires glow.

When fruit hangs heavy from the trees
    And a harvest moon shines bright,
Then wild geese form their perfect Vs
    In migratory flight.

When goldenrod and Queen Anne's lace
    Make bouquets on the hill,
Then Jack Frost shows his pixie face
    On every windowsill.

Then let each heart be filled with thanks
    For every bounteous yield
And sing a song of Autumn—
    Her promises fulfilled.

AUTUMN AFTERNOON
East Corinth, Vermont
Dick Dietrich Photography

Bright October

Kay Hoffman

I know no other season
   So filled with warmth and cheer
As on these bright October days
   When autumntime is here.

The hills have turned from summer's green
   To dazzling red and gold;
The flower beds are brighter too,
   So festive to behold!

The harvest yield is gathered in;
   God sends His gifts anew.
Each roadside stand, a harvest fair
   That warms the heart of you.

A bluish haze on distant hills,
   The maple's scarlet flame;
And oak trees dressed in Joseph-coats
   Stand guard along the lane.

Of all the seasons of the year,
   Each one with beauty blessed,
I hold to autumn's warmth and cheer—
   I like October best!

HARVEST GIFTS UNDER THE MAPLES
Moultonboro, New Hampshire
William Johnson/Johnson's Photography

Goldenrod

Annie Laurie Dunaway

Down a small country road,
I was traveling today;
And a hint of the autumn
Changed the scenes on my way.
For there on the banks,
Among rocks and clay clods;
My eyes looked with joy
On a lone goldenrod.

So rich was its color
As I looked at it there;
To describe it to others,
I hardly would dare.
A cluster of flowers
All joined on one stem,
And I glanced up ahead
To a garden of them.

I thought, as I lingered
And picked a bouquet,
Of the wonders of nature
That we see every day;
And I thought of the colors
Displayed in the woods,
Never captured on canvas—
No one ever could.

Still picking, I thought
Of the other flowers too
That grow in the forest
With various hues;
But here in the woodlands
Cultivated by God,
None bloom with such splendor
As the lone goldenrod.

Overleaf Photograph
BLACKBERRY CROSSING COVERED BRIDGE
White Mountain National Forest, New Hampshire
George Hunter/H. Armstrong Roberts

GOLDENROD AND KNAPWEED
Missisquoi National Wildlife Refuge, Vermont
William Johnson/Johnson's Photography

Swan Song

Rose Koralewsky

The long, bright flames of the goldenrod
Are blown aslant by the wind;
Blue sky shines through the elm trees
Where gilded leaves are thinned;
Softly the homing bluebird
Utters his plaintive call;
Over the drowsy hillsides
Lengthening shadows fall.

Soon with its trampling surges
Comes the wild autumn rain.
Flower and leaf and birdsong vanish;
But there remain
Memories of their beauty,
Garnered in precious store,
Living in hearts that love them
Till summer smiles once more.

SWANS AT WEQUETEQUOCK COVE
Pawcatuck, Connecticut
Dick Dietrich Photography

Readers' Reflections

HARVESTTIME REMINDS ME

The maple hills are splashed with gold and red,
And ripe, brown cattails border country roads.
The flaming apple trees bend low. Their fruit
Is ripe and waiting to be harvested.
At daybreak all the earth is blanched with frost.
Gray smoke curls up from chimneys once again.
I never cease to marvel how our God

Designed the world, not randomly, but sure
That every season does its part; and we
Have been instructed to take care of it.
The harvesttime reminds me of our gifts,
And I can say a grateful prayer of thanks.

Ruth J. Wahlberg
Two Harbors, Minnesota

COLD NOSE, WARM HEART

I walked the woods one wintry morn
And came upon a scene forlorn;
A little dog lay in the weeds,
A mixture of a dozen breeds.

This muddy, matted ball of fur,
Not knowing who his parents were,
No collar and no pedigree,
But seemed to like the likes of me.

He followed me back home that day;
With soulful eyes he asked to stay.
Now every night his favorite seat
Is close beside my slippered feet.

He's found the home he never knew.
He gives so much, his wants are few.
A friend arrived out of the storm
With nose so cold and heart so warm.

John W. Williams
DeWitt, Iowa

AUTUMN

Non-conformist of seasons,
Disheveler of nature,
Disturber of my peace,
You arouse once more
That sleeping gypsy in me.
Unleash my formulated life,
Unfetter my soul.
All of nature rebels with you
In one last protest
Against the white death of winter.
The leaves escape
Their bondage on the limb,
Fleeing responsibility.
But discontent to lie and rest,
They sweep along the earth
In a frenzied dance.
O wild days of autumn,
I rejoice secretly
In your erratic disorder
And find it hard to contain my spirit,
Yearning to be released,
To shout with the sounds of autumn,
To fly with the scattering leaves,
To sing with the sighing wind,
To float like a trail of pungent smoke
Wending its way to the misty heavens.

Betty Schumack
Winona, Minnesota

THANKSGIVING

I'm thankful for the autumn mist,
A sunrise giving earth a kiss,
A spider's web all drenched with dew
That sparkles when the light shines through.

I'm thankful for a forest green,
The singing of a silver stream,
The red and orange of maple trees
That softly drop their dying leaves.

I'm thankful for the evening's glow,
A fire slowly burning low,
For patterned geese against the sky
That honk their brief and faint good-bye.

I'm thankful for a harvest full
Of fruit that on strong branches pull,
For grain to make our daily bread
And all the bounties that we're fed.

I'm thankful for this time of year
That we can share with friends most dear,
And for a Father full of love
Who showers blessings from above.

LouAnn Mandzuik
Custer, Washington

Autumn Mischief

Emily Scarlett

Beyond the joys of August,
Through September's bright, blue days,
Awaits the Autumn's mischief child
In shadows where she plays.

Astride October's harvest winds,
Her laughter, loud and clear,
Leaves little doubt in any heart
Thanksgiving time is near!

She spreads an icy frosting
In the dawning's early morn,
Across the stubbled wheat field
And above the harvest corn.

For just a while she slows her pace
For Indian Summer's fun,
Then gently nudges her aside
To dim November's sun.

Alas, at times it slips her mind
That winter stays not warm,
And ofttimes she must hurry on
To flee December's storm!

AUTUMNTIME GIRL
Frances Hook, artist

Golden Peace

Patricia Sarazen

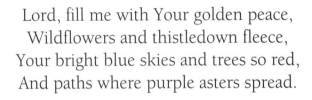

Lord, fill me with Your golden peace,
Wildflowers and thistledown fleece,
Your bright blue skies and trees so red,
And paths where purple asters spread.

To Your golden altar I will go;
Through silken, soft leaves, I will toe
Where scarlet maples lace the sky
And mountains reach above my eye.

Lord, fill me with the blithesome air,
The golds and reds just everywhere.
And I will follow the nomad bee
Where flowers bloom in ecstasy.

I'll travel to the golden peace
And watch the flight of many geese.
This autumn day, so bright and fair,
When trees hold gold within their hair.

16

ASPENS IN AUTUMN
Bad River Canyon, Copper Falls State Park
Ashland County, Wisconsin
Darryl R. Beers Photography

The Pace

THAT PASSES UNDERSTANDING

Mary E. Linton

Autumn is not a time designed for speed;
After the summer's careful ripening,
Moments of quiet are the spirit's need
And time to listen when the wood sprites sing,
Time to absorb the beauty and take home
Something to hold of blue October skies,
Gold leaves to hoard for days we cannot roam,
Colors that live on film when autumn dies.
Autumn is timed for little country roads
And hearts attuned to travel at their pace;
The four-lane speedways are for those who goad
All operations into one long race.
How much is lost—life's richest, highest power—
Tearing through the fall at sixty miles an hour.

And is an extra hour too much to spend
With all the countryside aflame with gold,
With rich fulfillment marking summer's end
And fall so soon a tale that has been told?
October woodlands cry for time to wait;
The beauty-wakened heart cries out to share
This wonderland before it is too late,
Before the frosty limbs stand gray and bare.
A few brief stops would make October mine
To have and hold when winter has begun.
This curve, that tree—the setting falls in line,
And all my soul cries out to be with one
Who stops for beauty, not to please my whim,
But from enthusiasm deep in Him.

SUGAR MAPLES IN PEAK COLOR
Huckleberry Lane, New Hampton, New Hampshire
William Johnson/Johnson's Photography

COUNTRY PUMPKINS. Original oil painting by Donald Zolan. © Zolan Fine Arts, Ltd. Hershey, Pennsylvania.

In Praise of Pumpkins

Craig E. Sathoff

Pumpkin bars and pumpkin bread
　　And spicy pumpkin pies
And pumpkin puddings, pumpkin cakes—
　　Oh, how they appetize!

The pumpkin is a cinch to grow:
　　Just three seeds to a hill,
The hills about three feet apart.
　　Five hills should reap your fill.

A lack of rain when blooms come on
　　Just might decrease your crop,
So get the hose and help them out
　　For harvests that are tops.

A jack-o-lantern is a must
　　When Halloween draws nigh;
So pick a pumpkin extra large,
　　Carve mouth and nose and eyes.

Then give to him a happy smile,
　　A really charming grin;
But remember what counts most, my friend—
　　The light that glows within.

From My Garden Journal
by Deana Deck
GOURDS

You can learn as much about gardening from your failures as from your successes. My first attempt to grow ornamental gourds, for example, was a total disaster. My plan was to harvest, cure, and varnish them for birdhouses and give them to friends for Christmas. Of course, my best laid plans don't always result in success!

Planting the gourds was easy. Most major gardening catalogs carry a selection of gourd seeds in the squash section, and many garden centers offer both seeds and plants in the spring. Both sources usually group all decorative gourds together under their common names. Most are actually of the *Lagenaria* genus which includes bottle gourds, dipper, calabash, and birdhouse gourds. *Cucurbita ficifolia* is a round, green and white gourd which is part of the cucumber family. A close relative is the *Cucurbita pepo* which produces small, hard gourds.

Wait until the soil is warm to plant gourds. If the nights are consistently in the 60° F range and days are in the mid- to high 70s, begin planting. By waiting until after the first of June to plant, you can avoid problems with squash vine borers. If you live in a northern climate, you'll need to start the seeds indoors four to five weeks before the last frost. Protect the plants from cool spring weather by keeping them containerized in a warm location until the soil is warm.

Gourds, squash, and tomatoes all require the same growing conditions: full sun, warm nights, lots of space (trellises and fences can help), and ample food and water. Add generous amounts of organic matter to the soil and two pounds of 5-10-10 fertilizer per fifty feet of row. Allow about ten feet of space between rows and at least three feet between plants in the row. Because gourd vines are prolific producers, you will only need four or five plants to assure a bountiful harvest.

Because the massive vines of the gourds I planted took up so much garden space, I was eager to harvest the gourds to make room for a fall planting of salad greens. As soon as the gourds appeared ripe, I cut them from the vines and carefully lined them up to dry on newspapers spread across a picnic table in my sunny backyard. That was my first mistake.

Then I merrily ripped out the invading vines and planted my cool season crops. Distracted by all this activity, I did not check on the gourds again for a couple of weeks; but when I did, it was a disappointing sight. Most had begun to rot, and others had developed telltale discolorations that indicated the only destination awaiting them was the compost pile. Birds had helped themselves to the seeds of the softest ones, and squirrels had purloined some of the smaller ones. I had no choice but to rethink my Christmas gift list.

A little research could have prevented a wasted growing season, but my college-educated, twentieth-century ego stood in the way. People were using gourds as bottles, dippers, bowls, spoons, and ladles for hundreds of years before the invention of pottery or glass. If primitive peoples could dry gourds, so could I, I reasoned—incorrectly, as it turned out.

My first mistake was to pick the gourds too early. They appeared ripe, but there's a difference between a ripe pumpkin or acorn squash and a ripe gourd. Both of the former are cousins to the gourd but are picked to be eaten fresh. A gourd which is to be dried needs to stay on the vine until the vine turns brown and begins to shrivel. It helps the color to place canning jar rings under the gourds to keep them off the ground as they ripen; it also prevents damp rot. You can achieve the same results by growing them on a tepee of stakes or along a fence or trellis.

If the first frost threatens before they're fully ripe, don't pick the gourds. Protect them with thick newspapers, burlap, or spun polyester row-cover fabric. Gourds which will be used for birdhouses, bottles, and dippers need from 140 to 150 days to reach maturity. If you have a short growing season in your area, start the seeds indoors several weeks before your last frost date.

Once the gourds are about to fall off the withered vines, remove them; leave about two inches of stem on each gourd to facilitate handling. Punch a hole in the top of the gourd to allow air to enter the cavity. Then thread a string or wire through this hole or a hole in the neck and use the string to hang the gourd away from the sun in a dry, well-ventilated space, such as an attic or a garage. Or place each gourd in a mesh onion or potato bag and hang it from a rafter. The gourds are ready for the next step if, when the gourds are shaken, the seeds inside rattle.

To make a birdhouse, cut a hole in the side of the gourd; make the hole the appropriate size for the type of bird you wish to attract. For bowls and other uses, cut the top off of the gourd with a small saw. Clean out the gourd and wash it thoroughly inside and out with alcohol or diluted bleach to help preserve it.

When the gourds are thoroughly dry, coat both the inside and outside with several coats of shellac or clear acrylic spray. Paint them if you would like to, but I prefer their natural colors. If you wish to use the gourds as birdhouses, do not put a perch on the outside. The birds don't need it, and it only helps curious cats and squirrels raid the nest.

Purple martins are especially fond of birdhouse gourds. These are highly social birds, however, who prefer close quarters. Hang at least eight gourds together, either along a wire or on yardarms nailed to a pole. The houses should be at least twelve feet off the ground, forty feet from any trees or other obstacles, and in an open lawn or meadow.

The entrance hole for a martin nest needs to be two-and-one-half inches in diameter and about one inch above the floor of the birdhouse. Ventilation is also important. As you can imagine, a gourd containing two parents and growing babies can heat up quickly on warm spring days. Drill a series of small holes in the neck of a long-necked gourd or on the upper sides of a round one. Place these ventilation holes at angles so they will admit air but not rain.

Even though my first crop of gourds ended up in the compost pile, I didn't give up. With a little bit of research, my next harvest proved successful, and my birdhouses were a big hit under the Christmas tree. Now, of course, everyone I know wants a gourd birdhouse next year!

Deana Deck tends to her flowers, plants, and vegetables at her home in Nashville, Tennessee, where her popular garden column is a regular feature in The Tennessean.

I'm Thankful for Each Day

Kay Hoffman

It matters not if rain or sun;
I'm thankful for each day that comes.
I open up my eyes and say,
"Oh, thank you, God, for another day."

Though once I thought I had to roam,
I'm now content right here at home.
No longer do I race about
Or think that I must hurry out.

So different from the work-a-day,
I view life in a simpler way.
Now that there's time to look around,
So many lovely things I've found.

A bird's nest in the apple tree
I watch with great expectancy
Till baby bird mouths open wide
For morsels mother bird provides.

A butterfly, a pretty rose,
A breeze that ruffles lines of clothes,
Bright blossom cups, a bumble bee
Is sipping nectar gingerly—

It matters not what may transcend,
I'm thankful for each day God sends.
I close my eyes at night and say,
"Oh, thank you, God, for a lovely day!"

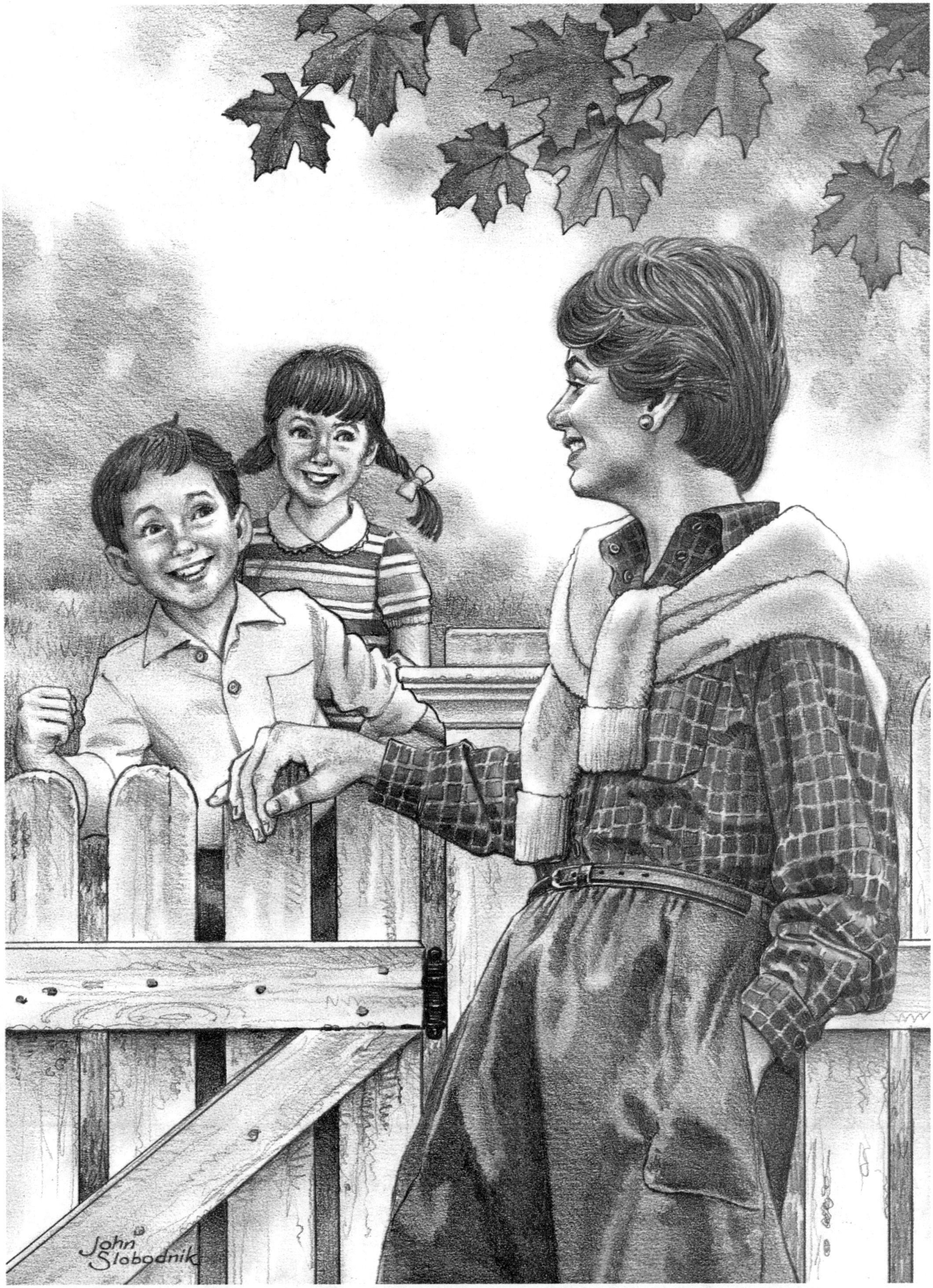
John
Slobodnik

A SLICE OF LIFE

Edgar A. Guest

GRATITUDE

Be grateful for the kindly friends
That walk along your way;
Be grateful for the skies of blue
That smile from day to day;

Be grateful for the health you own,
The work you find to do,
For round about you there are men
Less fortunate than you.

Be grateful for the growing trees,
    The roses soon to bloom,
The tenderness of kindly hearts
    That shared your days of gloom;
Be grateful for the morning dew,
    The grass beneath your feet,
The soft caresses of your babes
    And all their laughter sweet.

Acquire the grateful habit,
    Learn to see how blest you are,
How much there is to gladden life,
    How little life to mar!
And what if rain shall fall today
    And you with grief are sad;
Be grateful that you can recall
    The joys that you have had.

Edgar A. Guest began his illustrious career in 1895 at the age of fourteen when his work first appeared in the Detroit Free Press. *His column was syndicated in over three hundred newspapers, and he became known as "The Poet of the People."*

Patrick McRae is an artist who lives in the Milwaukee, Wisconsin, area. He has created nostalgic artwork for Ideals for more than a decade, and his favorite models are his wife and three children.

My Favorite Memory

Personal Stories of Treasured Memories from the Ideals Family of Readers

Thanksgiving Thoughts

As a child, I looked forward to the tastes and traditions of the Thanksgiving days in the 1920s that I spent at my grandparents' farm. As Thanksgiving Day approached, the goodies my grandmother would have waiting were all I could think about. My grandmother's preparations were made days before the occasion; and by the time we arrived, she had been up for hours. I would always head straight for the kitchen and watch her slowly remove the huge, brown turkey from the oven, my mouth watering from the tantalizing smell. Seeing my expression, my grandfather would try to break off a little piece to keep me from "starving," but my grandmother always thwarted his attempts with a smile on her face.

The table was a delight to the eye with its white linen tablecloth, shiny goblets, and monogrammed silver napkin rings that contrasted with my grandmother's blue and white china. Her old silver sugar and creamer dishes complemented the arrangement perfectly, as did the silver butter dish with a glass dome that appeared only on Thanksgiving.

After admiring the table, I would rush into the pantry, where I would find golden-crust pies of apple, mince, and squash plus a blueberry or banana cake.

After what seemed like hours, my grandfather, a wiry and energetic man, would call us to dinner. He was never happier than on Thanksgiving Day when he would carve the turkey and present the first leg to me. After the turkey was cut and served, my grandmother would bring out mounds of snowy white potatoes, creamy onions, her special chestnut dressing, green peas dripping with butter, and golden yellow squash. All the vegetables were homegrown on my grandparents' farm.

Throughout dinner, the adult conversation about crops and market prices did not interest me, and I would be thinking only of my favorite dessert. When the family had finally finished eating, I would go to the kitchen with my grandmother. We'd beat what seemed like dozens of eggs, add sugar to the yellow sauce until it became a thick, foamy white, then pour it over the Indian pudding.

Through the years I have tried many Indian puddings with that same sauce, but none have matched the rich, creamy taste that melted in my mouth when I was a child. Perhaps it is the twinkling of my grandmother's eyes, filled with pride, or the magic of childhood that is the missing ingredient!

Kathryn Libby
South Portland, Maine

Our First Thanksgiving

It was Thanksgiving Day 1952, and our small family had been invited to the home of our friends, the Mattsons. Coming from Norway six months before, I had no idea what Thanksgiving was or how it was celebrated, so when I walked into our friends' home and saw that bountiful table with the majestic golden turkey as the centerpiece, my mouth flew open. It was the grandest thing I had ever seen! We were served several vegetables in all kinds of hues—creamy potatoes, gravy, cranberry sauce, stuffing. All of us ate until our stomachs smarted, and then our hosts brought out the pies for dessert! I had never seen or tasted pie before, and I thought it was marvelous.

After dinner we helped with the dishes and then played several games with the Mattsons. They had five children and two grandchildren, so we were thirteen all together. Their family was very musical, so the festivities ended with songs, praise, and prayer.

I will never forget our first Thanksgiving in America and will always be thankful for the family who shared it with us.

Solveig Larson
Windsor, New York

Snow in Virginia

Every year on Thanksgiving, my family traveled from our home in northern Illinois to visit relatives in Virginia. My mother has three older brothers, so with all the grandchildren, aunts, and uncles, about twenty-five of us gathered at Grandma's house for dinner. We usually had the same meal every year—turkey, ham, scalloped oysters, mashed potatoes, dressing, green beans, corn, cranberry sauce, and yeast rolls. The number of pies depended on the number of people, but three favorites were always prepared—chocolate pie with fluffy meringue, chess pie, and pecan pie.

All of the kids would play in the backyard after dinner, each of us taking turns riding the silver gas tank like a wild bronco. One year, the day turned especially cold as it grew dark, and we went inside for cocoa dotted with tiny marshmallows. Exhausted from the day's excitement and warm from the cocoa, I fell asleep on the sofa while the adults talked in the kitchen. When it was time to go, my dad lifted me across his shoulder to carry me to the car, and I awoke outside in the midst of a winter wonderland. An early snow had blanketed the ground and frosted the bare-limbed trees.

It was one of those magical moments of childhood that I'll keep in my heart forever.

Edna Sutton
Rockford, Illinois

The Giant Pumpkin

The year we moved out of state for my husband's new job, we decided to spend Thanksgiving with my parents in Indiana since it would be a while before we could see them again. Soon after we arrived, my daughter, Jeanette, came running into the kitchen. "Mommy, come look at the giant pumpkin!" she squealed. Once outside, I saw the two-foot-tall, three-foot-wide vegetable in my mother's garden. The children were having a wonderful time taking turns sitting on top of the pumpkin, so I got my camera and took a snapshot of each child posing on the huge, orange ball.

Our extended family was able to get together a few more times over the years; and each time we visited, my mother had the pumpkin pictures on display on her corkboard in the kitchen, next to the doorway notched with two generations of heights. Visits and reunions have become too few, and it is the memories that help me feel a sense of family while we are apart. Years later, Mother gave the pumpkin pictures to me; today they are kept in a scrapbook that holds special memories of our family.

Andrea Zywicki
Decatur, Indiana

Editor's Note: Do you have a holiday or seasonal memory that you'd like to share with the Ideals *family of readers? Send your typed memory to:*

MY FAVORITE MEMORY
C/O EDITORIAL DEPARTMENT
IDEALS MAGAZINE
535 METROPLEX DRIVE, SUITE 250
NASHVILLE, TENNESSEE 37211

Thanksgiving

Charles Hanson Towne

The fevered meadow and the road
And the rain's healing hands that bless,
Lord, I give thanks
For the green gospel of the grass,
And the white billowy clouds that pass;
For the world's great loveliness,
Whereon is set my still abode.
I thank Thee for the quiet moon,
Long shadows in the afternoon;
For the great peace the blue sky knows,
And the red raiment of the rose;
For the soft tumult of the leaves,
For the clear sky on wind-blown nights,
And all the little village lights
That smile at me through winter's dark,
Each on a human, tender spark.
For apple orchards, white with May,
For many a far sequestered way;

For the deep patience of the pool
Within a forest beautiful.
I thank Thee for the simple things,
Beyond the glory of the kings;
For goodly books to read at night
In a sweet peace of candlelight;
For bread to break, a child to kiss
And O, dear Lord, for this and this;
The love of woman that shall last
Till time itself and life have passed.
And as the long bright journey ends,
Lord, I give thanks for many friends.

THROUGH MY WINDOW

Pamela Kennedy
Art by Ron Adair

AN AMERICAN THANKSGIVING

Every morning at eight o'clock I hear "The Star-Spangled Banner" as it echoes over the naval station where we live. At sunset, cars, trucks, pedestrians, children at play, even guests at outdoor receptions stop whatever they are doing and remain silent while "Evening Colors" rings in the darkening sky. Accompanying these events, flags are raised or lowered on ships and flagpoles. It is a normal part of our daily rhythm here, but I always enjoy the reactions of our guests, many of whom have no associations with the military. Invariably they wonder what is going on, then straighten with pride when they realize they are wit-

nessing a time-honored ceremony older than our country. For a few moments they have the opportunity to demonstrate their appreciation for our flag, the symbol of their citizenship.

It is good, I think, to give thanks for our country in both large and small ways. I know there are many who point out its shortcomings, but they couldn't even do that without the freedoms America allows. I am thankful for a country that permits discourse and disagreements, for these encourage us to exercise and stretch our democratic muscles and become stronger in the process. I am thankful for the diversity of choice I am allowed; from the kind of breakfast cereal I buy to the types of literature I read. Whether my neighbors are Christian, Jewish, Islamic, Buddhist, or New Age, I am thankful they can practice their beliefs without fear of governmental reprisal. I am thankful my children have friends of varied ethnic backgrounds and have learned to respect rather than ridicule those of different nationalities.

For those who have lost this sense of thankfulness or are, perhaps, discouraged by the popularity of pessimism, I suggest a trip abroad. A few years ago, my mother and I took a short vacation to Hong Kong. At each stop along the way, we went through the ritual of customs checks and passport inspections. It became clear that my small, navy blue passport was the most valuable document in my possession. Without it I would be denied entrance or exit. Even though I knew all was in order, I experienced a bit of tension each time I handed it to a stern-faced customs inspector. Every time it was approved, stamped, and returned to me, I felt relief—and a bit of pride at being an American citizen.

One evening, as we shopped in a crowded store on a side street in Kowloon, Mother turned to me in panic. "Someone stole my wallet!" Despite her precautions, in the crush of shoppers, someone had unzipped her purse, reached in, and removed her wallet containing her travelers' checks, cash, and passport. The checks could be replaced and the cash was negligible, but the loss of the passport loomed as a major catastrophe. Our departing flight left in thirty-six hours!

Nothing could be done that night, but at eight A.M. I was on the phone to the American consulate. They assured me the passport could be replaced with proper documentation of citizenship, so we headed across Hong Kong harbor feeling a little like women without a country.

As we climbed the steep sidewalk leading to the consulate building, we saw block-long lines of people apparently waiting to gain entrance. It was a warm, muggy day, and I didn't relish the thought of standing in the heat for hours, so I approached the heavily armed guard to ask if there was somewhere Mother could sit while we waited.

"Are you Americans?" he asked. When I said we were, he motioned us toward a locked gate. "You don't need to wait in line. These people are here hoping to get visas to go to the United States. They aren't citizens. You go in through here." He produced a key and guided us into the courtyard. Once inside, we were escorted past another group of folks who were waiting for the next step in the visa process. Eventually we were handed off to a third guard who led us to an office upstairs where we would wait to be interviewed by a consulate officer.

As we waited, I thought about all those people anxious to come to the United States, each one hoping to qualify for a visa. Many waited years, applying again and again. Mother's lost passport seemed even more valuable in the light of their quest. When our turn for an interview arrived, a pleasant woman greeted us and asked Mother to explain how the passport was lost. When the story was finished, we were both asked several other questions to verify our citizenship. I had to make a written statement attesting to the validity of our claim and surrender my own passport for examination and tracing. When all was in order, Mother paid the replacement fee, was photographed, and received her new passport.

Leaving the consulate, we walked past the lines of people, the weary families with crying babies, the armed guards, and stood for a moment looking up at the American flag floating in the sultry breeze. It was more beautiful than I remembered.

Now when I hear the national anthem in the morning or "Colors" at sunset, I recall that flag and others like it all over the world. It is just a piece of cloth some say, a symbol, an old-fashioned statement of outdated patriotism. But it rises over military bases, embassies, and consulates; it hangs on front porches and parades through city streets because people recognize the priceless gift for which it stands. And they are, as I am, very thankful to be an American.

Pamela Kennedy is a freelance writer of short stories, articles, essays, and children's books. Wife of a naval officer and mother of three children, she has made her home on both U.S. coasts and currently resides in Honolulu, Hawaii. She draws her material from her own experiences and memories, adding highlights from her imagination to enhance the story.

As We Approach This Season

Georgia B. Adams

As we approach this season,
We thank Thee, gracious Lord,
For harvests truly bountiful
And every rich reward.

We thank Thee for the blessings
Inherited this year,
For love of friends and family
And all of those held dear.

We're solemnly reflecting
Upon Thy tender love,
Thy hand of grace and mercy
Extended from above.

As we approach this season,
Dear Lord, we pray that we
May realize Thy mercies
And give our praise to Thee.

Giving Thanks

J. Pat Babin

We bow our heads in humble thanks
For every gift and blessing,
For those who gather here to share
Our turkey and the dressing.
But most of all we're thankful for
This great land of the free
Where we can recognize our God
And worship openly.

NINETEENTH-CENTURY HOUSE
Jessie Walker Associates

OUR HERITAGE

A NATIONAL PRAYER

Thomas Jefferson

Almighty God, Who has given us this good land for our heritage, we humbly beseech Thee that we may always prove ourselves a people mindful of Thy favor and glad to do Thy will. Bless our land with honorable industry, sound learning, and pure manners.

Save us from violence, discord and confusion, from pride and arrogance, and from every evil way. Defend our liberties, and fashion into one united people the multitude brought hither out of many kindreds and tongues.

Endow with the spirit of wisdom those to whom in Thy Name we entrust the authority of government, that there may be justice and peace at home, and that through obedience to Thy law, we may show forth Thy praise among the nations of the earth.

In time of prosperity, fill our hearts with thankfulness, and, in the day of trouble, suffer not our trust in Thee to fail; all of which we ask through Jesus Christ our Lord. AMEN.

ABOUT THE AUTHOR

One of America's most remarkable leaders, Thomas Jefferson was born on April 13, 1743, in Shadwell, Virginia. Educated at the College of William and Mary, he practiced law and served in the Virginia House of Burgesses before being elected to the Continental Congress. In 1776, Jefferson became the nation's voice when the Congress chose him to write the Declaration of Independence. He went on to serve as Virginia's governor, the U.S. minister to France, secretary of state under George Washington, and vice president under John Adams. In 1801, the American people chose Jefferson to be the country's third president. His most notable accomplishments during his two terms were the acquisition of the Louisiana Territory from Napoleon in 1803 and the organization and support of the Lewis and Clark expedition. After his retirement from office, Jefferson helped form the core of the Library of Congress by selling his extensive collection of books to the government; and, as his last great public service, he spearheaded the founding of the University of Virginia at the age of seventy-six. Thomas Jefferson died on July 4, 1826, the fifty-year anniversary of the Declaration of Independence.

—Andrea Zywicki

Thanksgiving Proclamation of 1863

Abraham Lincoln

It has seemed to me fit and proper that [the gifts of God] should be solemnly, reverently, and gratefully acknowledged with one heart and one voice by the whole American people. I do, therefore, invite my fellow citizens . . . to set apart and observe the last Thursday of November next as a day of thanksgiving and praise to our beneficent Father who dwelleth in the heavens.

THANKSGIVING THOUGHTS

Ruby Jourdan Hillix

The Pilgrims had so little,
    Yet they humbly gave their thanks
For food and warmth and shelter
    And for peace within their ranks.

We take these things for granted
    And enjoy them every day—
Our freedom and our families
    And the chance to work and play.

So as our prayers are offered,
    May we look into our hearts
And thank God for the blessings
    That have set this day apart.

TRAVELER'S Diary

Andrea Zywicki

MONTICELLO
Near Charlottesville, Virginia

I have always loved beautiful, historic houses, and I never miss an opportunity to tour one. So when my husband and I traveled to the Washington, D.C., area for our annual autumn vacation, I made sure we scheduled a stop at Monticello, the impressive mountaintop home of Thomas Jefferson.

Being a bit of a history buff, I read up on the famous domicile before our trip. I was surprised to learn that Jefferson originally built Monticello (so named for its Italian translation, *little mountain*) in 1782 but then tore most of it down seven years later and started all over. After spending four years serving as the U.S. minister to France from 1785 until 1789, Jefferson was inspired to renovate the house again; he had to make room for the eighty-six crates of new furnishings he shipped back from France. In fact, Jefferson became so engrossed in the constant renovations of Monticello throughout his life that he accrued substantial debt. When he died in 1826, his daughter, Martha, was forced to sell the house, its contents, and the surrounding farms to pay her father's debts.

The Thomas Jefferson Memorial Foundation took title to Monticello in 1923 and began giving tours of this famous dwelling. Since the Foundation could not recover all of Jefferson's possessions, it has had to supplement with reproductions. As I walked through the rooms of Monticello, I was impressed by the authentic atmosphere of yesteryear that the Foundation has reproduced in the elegantly appointed rooms, but what fascinated me more than anything were the numerous architectural wonders throughout the house. Jefferson was an inventor at heart, and Monticello features several of his creative endeavors.

Jefferson was especially intrigued by inventions that used time, light, and energy efficiently, and the Great Clock in the entrance hall of Monticello aptly exemplifies this aspect of his genius. Jefferson designed the seven-day clock in 1792 in an on-going campaign to improve order on his estate. I was surprised to see that the clock has two faces, one on the inside of the house and one outside on the east front of the house. Even more unusual, however, is the elaborate mechanism by which the clock runs. Two sets of cannon-ball weights descend into holes in the floor on either side of the clock as the seconds tick past. Labels placed on the wall along the path of the weights indicate the days of the week, except for Friday afternoon and Saturday, which disappear down into the cellar (Jefferson ran out of room). There they remain until the clock is rewound on Sunday.

Since Jefferson regarded grand staircases as expensive and space-wasting, he designed two extremely narrow staircases on either side of the entrance hall to provide access to the upper floor. As I viewed the steep steps of the twenty-four-inch-wide stairwell, I began to think perhaps Jefferson had gone too far in his pursuit of efficiency. Tours are restricted to the ground floor, however, so I didn't have to test my athletic ability after all. I proceeded on to Jefferson's own quarters, which were thankfully on the ground floor.

During Jefferson's travels in France, he delighted in the space-saving qualities of the alcove beds he saw there and incorporated the same design into the bedrooms of Monticello. Jefferson's bedroom features an alcove bed that is open on both sides, with walls only at the head and foot of the bed. This situates his bed between his bedroom and his study, which served as his summertime "oval office" during his tenure as president.

Although I came to Monticello to see a beautiful home and learn of its history, I also learned a great deal about the remarkable man behind it. Jefferson's Monticello stands today as an impressive testament to his inventive genius and good taste. As I walked away from the "little mountain" at the end of my tour, I felt very much as if I'd walked through a piece of American history.

Hymn

Lucy Larcom

Written for the two hundredth anniversary of the Old South Church, Beverly, Massachusetts

The sea sang sweetly to the shore
   Two hundred years ago:
To weary Pilgrim ears it bore
   A welcome, deep and low.

They gathered, in the autumnal calm,
   To their first house of prayer;
And softly rose their Sabbath psalm
   On the wild woodland air.

The ocean took the echo up;
   It rang from tree to tree:
And praise, as from an incense cup,
   Poured over earth and sea.

They linger yet upon the breeze,
   The hymns our fathers sung:
They rustle in the roadside trees
   And give each leaf a tongue.

The grand old sea is moaning yet
   With music's mighty pain:
No chorus has arisen to fit
   Its wondrous anthem-strain.

When human hearts are tuned to Thine,
   Whose voice is in the sea,
Life's murmuring waves a song divine
   Shall chant, O God, to Thee!

MAYFLOWER II
Plymouth Harbor, Plymouth, Massachusetts
William Johnson/Johnson's Photography

The New Colossus

Emma Lazarus

Not like the brazen giant of Greek fame,
With conquering limbs astride from land to land,
Here at our sea-washed, sunset gates shall stand
A mighty woman with a torch, whose flame
Is the imprisoned lightning, and her name
Mother of Exiles. From her beacon-hand
Glows world-wide welcome; her mild eyes command
The air-bridged harbor that twin cities frame.
"Keep, ancient lands, your storied pomp!" cries she
With silent lips. "Give me your tired, your poor,
Your huddled masses yearning to breathe free,
The wretched refuse of your teeming shore.
Send these, the homeless, tempest-tost to me,
I lift my lamp beside the golden door!"

Inscription on the Statue of Liberty:
This tablet, with her Sonnet to the Bartholdi Statue of Liberty
engraved upon it, is placed upon these walls in loving memory of
Emma Lazarus
born in New York City, July 22, 1849
Died November 18, 1887

THE STATUE OF LIBERTY
New York, New York
Dianne Dietrich Leis

LEGENDARY AMERICANS

NANCY J. SKARMEAS

EMMA LAZARUS

The poet Emma Lazarus was born in New York City in 1849, one of seven children of Moses and Esther Lazarus, whose families had immigrated to America from Portugal in the 1600s. The Lazarus family was wealthy and secure; and the children, especially the six daughters, grew up in a sheltered, insular world. They were educated at home by private tutors and saw little of the city outside their own doorstep. Young Emma Lazarus studied the classics, art, music, and history and wrote poetry. Generations removed from her own immigrant ancestors, she had never imagined a connection between herself and the flood of immigrants that daily swelled New York's poorer neighborhoods; yet Emma Lazarus became a dedicated champion of all those who sought refuge and renewal on American soil.

Emma Lazarus completed her first book of poetry when she was just seventeen years old and published a second volume four years later. Beginning in her teens, she corresponded regularly with the great American author Ralph Waldo Emerson, and in her twenties she penned poems for the leading literary magazines of the day and published a novel. Yet when Emerson compiled an anthology of American poetry in 1874, he did not include his young friend's work. Another correspondent may have revealed to Lazarus the reason why. He wrote to her that for her poetry to have true depth and the power to move its readers, she must write from "the overflowing of a life rich in other ways." A child of wealth and privilege, the daughter of an over-protective father, Emma was a bright and sensitive young woman with a rich inner life, yet her words could not break down the walls that surrounded her and touch the hearts of those she could not see and did not know.

Oddly enough, it was a series of events on the other side of the world that finally tore down the walls surrounding Emma Lazarus. In 1881, Czar Alexander II of Russia was assassinated, and his country erupted into violent chaos. Russian Jews became the victims of horrendous persecution, and thousands fled their homeland seeking refuge in America. As the refugees began arriving in New York City, word of their suffering spread throughout the city. Among those moved by the plight of these refugees was a thirty-one-year-old poet named Emma Lazarus, herself a descendant of Jewish immigrants. After hearing a speech describing the horrors of the Russian pogroms, Lazarus took up her well-practiced pen and began writing, for the first time in her life, with a true sense of purpose. She began to write poems, essays, articles, and even a play, all denouncing the persecution of the Jews in Russia and of oppressed people worldwide.

At about the same time that Lazarus took up the cause of Russia's refugees, another New Yorker, newspaper publisher Joseph Pulitzer, himself an immigrant from Hungary, was taking up a cause of his own. In 1883, the Statue of Liberty, a gift from the nation of France to the American people meant to symbolize the two nations' shared love of liberty, stood in Paris awaiting transport to New York Harbor. In the United States, funds were being raised to finance the construction of a pedestal on which Lady Liberty would stand, but the public had proved themselves ambivalent and uninspired. What did this odd gift represent, people wondered? What purpose would this statue serve? American citizens outside New York thought the money should come from the people of New York City; the poor believed financing was the responsibility of the rich; and the wealthy hesitated also, wondering if this statue—given by the revolutionary French—represented some sort of symbolic threat to their security. Joseph Pulitzer wrote editorials blasting the people of America for not supporting the statue, and he began a personal crusade to raise the money necessary to bring Liberty to America.

One of Pulitzer's fund-raising schemes involved a poetry contest, and one entry was a poem called "The New Colossus," written in 1883 by Emma Lazarus. The poem gave a new name to the statue that its French sculptor had called "Liberty Enlightening the World." Lazarus called her the "Mother of Exiles" and imagined her light as a welcoming beacon offering comfort and safety to all who sought refuge. Mr. Pulitzer's campaign was a success, and he ultimately helped rally the American people behind the Statue of Liberty project. Emma Lazarus's poem helped Americans come to an understanding of what the statue meant to them, and what it would mean to the world.

Emma Lazarus died of a tragic illness only four years after writing "The New Colossus." She was only thirty-eight years old. In the final six years of her life she had been an impassioned spokeswoman for persecuted people worldwide, and she had worked hard to establish a network of support for refugees coming to America from every corner of the globe. But Emma Lazarus is remembered best for her connection to the Statue of Liberty. In 1903, "The New Colossus" was inscribed on the interior wall of the pedestal beneath the Statue of Liberty, and today the poem and the statue are inseparable in the minds and hearts of people the world over. Emma Lazarus, her heart expanded by her empathy for exiled Russian immigrants, used her poetry to reach out to exiles and refugees from every walk of life; from her deep compassion flowed the words of "The New Colossus," words that have proven truly immortal.

Another Thanksgiving

Elizabeth Ann M. Moore

For all the beauties of the earth,
For harmonies of mind,
For art and music on the wind,
The art of being kind,
For healing many broken hearts,
The lessons patience brings,
The silent splendor of the soul
On meditation's wings,
For friends and family and joy,
Forgiveness, peace, and prayer,
For everything we offer, Lord,
Thanksgiving everywhere.

Scarecrow

Ruth Smoker

The harvest has been gathered in;
And with your rakish pose,
You guarded well the precious grain
Against sly, thieving crows.

Silent, brainless sentinel
With eyes that cannot see,
Congratulations for your work
Performed unknowingly.

MORNING IN THE WHEAT FIELD
Lake Placid, New York
William Johnson/Johnson's Photography

Psalm 136

O Give thanks unto the Lord;
    for he is good: for his mercy endureth for ever.
O give thanks unto the God of gods:
    for his mercy endureth for ever.
O give thanks to the Lord of lords:
    for his mercy endureth for ever.
To him who alone doeth great wonders:
    for his mercy endureth for ever.
To him that by wisdom made the heavens:
    for his mercy endureth for ever.
To him that stretched out the earth above the waters:
    for his mercy endureth for ever.
To him that made great lights:
    for his mercy endureth for ever:
The sun to rule by day:
    for his mercy endureth for ever:
The moon and stars to rule by night:
    for his mercy endureth for ever.

PSALM 136:1–9

Devotions FROM THE Heart

Pamela Kennedy

"And whatsoever ye do in word or deed, do all in the name of the Lord Jesus,
giving thanks to God and the Father by him."

Colossians 3:17

DOING IT ALL FOR HIM

The cleaning lady at the school came after the children left and worked by herself. She was not fast, but she was very thorough. Carefully she swept the rooms in the small school, emptied the waste baskets, removed the errant paper airplanes from atop the cloak closets, and polished the windows. When she left each room, she paused in the doorway, nodded with satisfaction, and murmured, "there you go." Month after month, year after year, she faithfully did the most menial chores. When asked if she ever tired of cleaning for the schoolchildren, she replied, "I surely would, if I were doing it for them. But I'm not." Then she smiled, and a twinkle lit up her eyes. She pointed toward the ceiling and leaned close before whispering, "I'm doing it for Him. It's my way of saying thanks for all His blessings."

This woman understood a great principle: a grateful heart is a powerful motivator. How easy it is to see what we do as unimportant, especially if the task is repetitive. The homemaker who cleans bathrooms that only get dirty again, spends hours preparing meals that are consumed in a few minutes, and does countless tasks each day without any recognition finds it easy to become discouraged. The office worker who repeats the same routine at the same desk week after week knows how difficult it is to feel fulfilled. Life isn't a thrill a minute for most of us. Frequently we become discouraged and bored; sometimes we question what we're doing or even why we're here!

What would happen, I wonder, if we adopted the cleaning lady's philosophy? Instead of cleaning or working for the family or the boss, how would we change if we "did it for Him?" If we looked at each task before us as a gift to God, would it matter if others didn't appreciate it? If our efforts poured from an attitude of gratitude instead of grim determination, wouldn't our work take on a new meaning?

When Paul wrote to the believers in Colosse, he was not writing to people who had exciting careers in a progressive society. Most of them lived below the poverty level and were subject to the whims of an oppressive government. Yet he enjoined them to speak and act from hearts filled with thanksgiving to God. Doesn't it seem a bit contradictory? Perhaps that is because we have come to understand thanksgiving as the act of expressing gratitude for material blessings alone. The early Christians recognized a wealth their society neither saw nor understood. They had the joy of knowing the love of other believers, the deep comfort of fellowship. They experienced the forgiveness and cleansing only God could offer and the resulting peace of mind and heart that passed all understanding. In the words of God, in psalms and songs, they enjoyed the ecstacy of praise that lifted their tired spirits from the mundane world in which they lived. They knew the security of being a beloved child of God, rescued for eternity by His Son. No wonder they could give thanks in word and deed! Their lives were restricted and narrow only in a physical sense. Spiritually, they enjoyed the unlimited breadth and height and length of the kingdom of God!

Perhaps this Thanksgiving we can learn the simple lesson of the cleaning lady. Perhaps we can start doing it all for Him.

Dear God, when I become discouraged and find it hard to be thankful for my daily routine,
please help me to focus on how You have blessed me. Let all my words and actions be motivated
by a thankful heart. Help me to do it all for You. AMEN.

BITS & PIECES

O for a thousand tongues to sing my great
Redeemer's praise.
—*Charles Wesley*

*T*hank you, Lord, for the sheer joy of wanting
to get up and help the world go around.
—*Roxie Gibson*

*T*hanksgiving was never meant to be shut up in a single day.
—*Robert Caspar Lintner*

*T*he Lord gives His blessing when He finds the vessel empty.
—*Thomas á Kempis*

*T*hy bounty shines in autumn unconfined,
And spreads a common feast for all that lives.
—*James Thomson*

*J*ust the word *thanksgiving* prompts the spirit of humility.
Genuine gratitude to God for His mercy, His abundance,
His protection, His smile of favor. Life simplifies itself.
—*Charles R. Swindoll*

*R*eflect upon your present blessings of which every man
has many; not on your past misfortunes of which all
men have some.
—*Charles Dickens*

*O*n earth join all ye creatures to extol Him first,
Him last, Him midst, and without end.
—*John Milton*

Thanksgiving Time

Elisabeth Weaver Winstead

The sound of merry laughter
    Fills our home this holiday.
We feast on nature's bounty
    In a tempting, bright array.

Our cousins, aunts, and uncles
    Are all gathered by the score
To celebrate Thanksgiving Day;
    We could not ask for more.

This treasured harvest feast is shared
    By those we cherish best;
With happy hearts we bow our heads
    In gratitude expressed.

Then when the day is over
    And it's time for guests to part,
The spirit of Thanksgiving
    Lingers still within each heart.

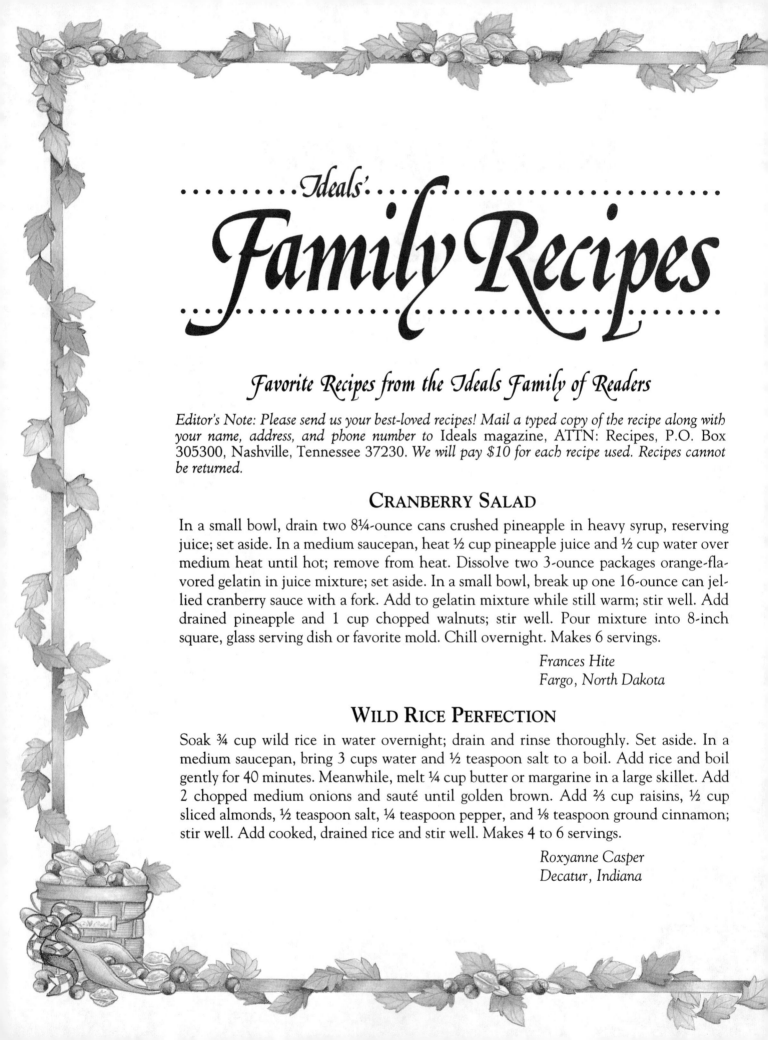

Ideals' Family Recipes

Favorite Recipes from the Ideals Family of Readers

Editor's Note: Please send us your best-loved recipes! Mail a typed copy of the recipe along with your name, address, and phone number to Ideals magazine, ATTN: Recipes, P.O. Box 305300, Nashville, Tennessee 37230. We will pay $10 for each recipe used. Recipes cannot be returned.

CRANBERRY SALAD

In a small bowl, drain two 8¼-ounce cans crushed pineapple in heavy syrup, reserving juice; set aside. In a medium saucepan, heat ½ cup pineapple juice and ½ cup water over medium heat until hot; remove from heat. Dissolve two 3-ounce packages orange-flavored gelatin in juice mixture; set aside. In a small bowl, break up one 16-ounce can jellied cranberry sauce with a fork. Add to gelatin mixture while still warm; stir well. Add drained pineapple and 1 cup chopped walnuts; stir well. Pour mixture into 8-inch square, glass serving dish or favorite mold. Chill overnight. Makes 6 servings.

Frances Hite
Fargo, North Dakota

WILD RICE PERFECTION

Soak ¾ cup wild rice in water overnight; drain and rinse thoroughly. Set aside. In a medium saucepan, bring 3 cups water and ½ teaspoon salt to a boil. Add rice and boil gently for 40 minutes. Meanwhile, melt ¼ cup butter or margarine in a large skillet. Add 2 chopped medium onions and sauté until golden brown. Add ⅔ cup raisins, ½ cup sliced almonds, ½ teaspoon salt, ¼ teaspoon pepper, and ⅛ teaspoon ground cinnamon; stir well. Add cooked, drained rice and stir well. Makes 4 to 6 servings.

Roxyanne Casper
Decatur, Indiana

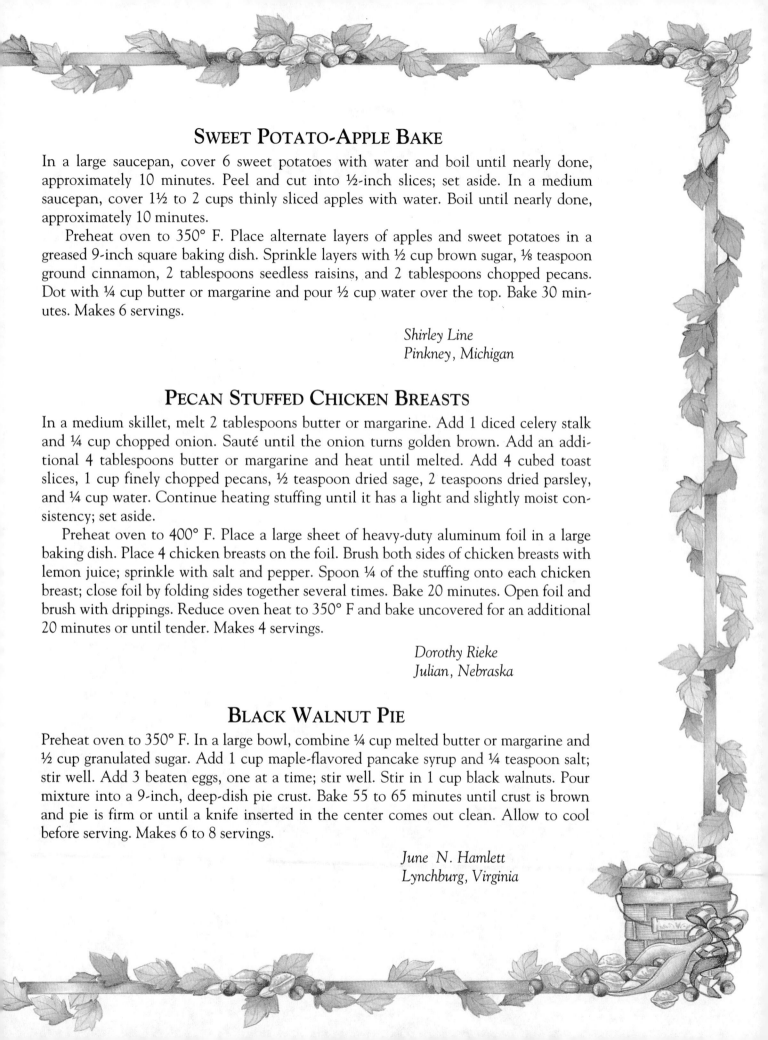

SWEET POTATO-APPLE BAKE

In a large saucepan, cover 6 sweet potatoes with water and boil until nearly done, approximately 10 minutes. Peel and cut into ½-inch slices; set aside. In a medium saucepan, cover 1½ to 2 cups thinly sliced apples with water. Boil until nearly done, approximately 10 minutes.

Preheat oven to 350° F. Place alternate layers of apples and sweet potatoes in a greased 9-inch square baking dish. Sprinkle layers with ½ cup brown sugar, ⅛ teaspoon ground cinnamon, 2 tablespoons seedless raisins, and 2 tablespoons chopped pecans. Dot with ¼ cup butter or margarine and pour ½ cup water over the top. Bake 30 minutes. Makes 6 servings.

Shirley Line
Pinkney, Michigan

PECAN STUFFED CHICKEN BREASTS

In a medium skillet, melt 2 tablespoons butter or margarine. Add 1 diced celery stalk and ¼ cup chopped onion. Sauté until the onion turns golden brown. Add an additional 4 tablespoons butter or margarine and heat until melted. Add 4 cubed toast slices, 1 cup finely chopped pecans, ½ teaspoon dried sage, 2 teaspoons dried parsley, and ¼ cup water. Continue heating stuffing until it has a light and slightly moist consistency; set aside.

Preheat oven to 400° F. Place a large sheet of heavy-duty aluminum foil in a large baking dish. Place 4 chicken breasts on the foil. Brush both sides of chicken breasts with lemon juice; sprinkle with salt and pepper. Spoon ¼ of the stuffing onto each chicken breast; close foil by folding sides together several times. Bake 20 minutes. Open foil and brush with drippings. Reduce oven heat to 350° F and bake uncovered for an additional 20 minutes or until tender. Makes 4 servings.

Dorothy Rieke
Julian, Nebraska

BLACK WALNUT PIE

Preheat oven to 350° F. In a large bowl, combine ¼ cup melted butter or margarine and ½ cup granulated sugar. Add 1 cup maple-flavored pancake syrup and ¼ teaspoon salt; stir well. Add 3 beaten eggs, one at a time; stir well. Stir in 1 cup black walnuts. Pour mixture into a 9-inch, deep-dish pie crust. Bake 55 to 65 minutes until crust is brown and pie is firm or until a knife inserted in the center comes out clean. Allow to cool before serving. Makes 6 to 8 servings.

June N. Hamlett
Lynchburg, Virginia

Holiday Feast

Bonnie T. O'Brien

The air is crisp and trees are gold;
A glowing fire turns the cold.
The kitchen pours out scents so sweet,
And someone shouts, "It's time to eat!"

So, say the blessing, Father dear.
Come, Grandpa, you sit over here.
Sister, pass the relish plate.
Now sit down, Mother, don't be late.

Radish roses, celery sticks—
Pass the mashed potatoes, quick.
Steaming dressing piled high—
Save room for the pumpkin pie!

Turkey, chicken, ham, and such,
Gravy with Mom's golden touch,
Candles burning, hearts aglow—
Holidays may come and go;

But, oh! The look and smells of fall—
Thanksgiving dinner best of all!

Bountiful Blessings

Mildred L. Jarrell

I'm thankful for the bright blue sky
I raise my eyes to see
And for the rich dark earth I sow,
The fruit it yields for me.

I'm thankful for our daily bread,
Each dear one round the board,
And for the tie of heav'nly love
That binds us in accord.

I'm thankful for the gentle rain
That greens the grassy leas,
The gift of gold to each of us
From Autumn as she flees.

I'm thankful for our cottage small
Where hearth is warm and bright,
And for the peaceful comfort here—
A haven in the night.

I'm thankful for our blessings too,
Though they be great or small,
And for a loving God on high
Who watches over all.

HANDMADE HEIRLOOM

CREWEL NEEDLEPOINT TABLECLOTH. Crafted by Mary Skarmeas. Jerry Koser Photography.

CREWEL NEEDLEPOINT
Mary Skarmeas

This Thanksgiving, our table will be set for twelve. It's funny; after years of a family that seemed to be shrinking as our children grew and moved on to lives of their own, we are growing again as grandchildren fill our lives. We will sit down to the traditional meal of turkey and stuffing and cranberries and pies, the china dishes will be those familiar from years of use, and even

64

the conversation, I am sure, will have a familiar ring as old favorite stories are recounted once more. But there will be one thing new. This year, I will cover the table with a new linen tablecloth, with corners adorned by crewel embroidery. I worked on this tablecloth in the quiet spring afternoons as my granddaughter Alex slept upstairs. Maybe nobody else will notice, not right away. But I hope that in years to come my new tablecloth will seem as old and familiar as the talk across the family table.

Crewel work is, quite simply, wool yarn embroidery on linen. The yarn—a two-ply, worsted wool—is worked with a sharp embroidery needle in non-geometric, free-flowing patterns. The art is ancient; examples exist from Egypt and the northeastern Mediterranean from the fourth century. But crewel work came to America by way of England, where the craft flourished in the sixteenth and seventeenth centuries. Mary Queen of Scots was among the more illustrious of British women who passed their leisure time adorning bedding, draperies, and clothing with crewel embroidery. The appeal was in the simplicity and flexibility of the art. Crewel work did not require total coverage of the fabric background with stitching; instead, it was like sketching on paper. A bed coverlet was as manageable as a tiny handkerchief when only the borders or maybe even only the corners were to be stitched with flowers, leaves, fruits, birds, or other simple designs. When British settlers came to America, they brought their crewel skills with them and found inspiration for designs in the native plants, flowers, trees, and fruits of their new land.

Crewel embroidery employs a variety of stitches, most often the crewel or outline stitch, along with brick, long-and-short, buttonhole, French knot, brick-and-cross, and a variety of other decorative and filler stitches. The needles are sharp, and the fabric should be linen or linen blend. Only authentic crewel wool should be used—the texture and colors are rich, and the yarn is durable. The fabric can be held by hand, but it is best secured in a frame or hoop.

I created the design for my tablecloth from a group of simple line-art flowers and leaves cut from various sources, including a clip art book and a child's coloring book. I cut out each element and then experimented with layout on paper until I decided on the design I wanted. I then used tracing paper and transfer paper to apply the designs to the tablecloth corners. Crewel work is by nature free-flowing. There are no hard and fast rules about layout and design; simply do what pleases your eye. It is in the design elements you choose, the beautiful, rich colors of the wool, and the skill of the stitching that crewel work shines.

Thanksgiving at our house is a casual affair. We don't own fine china or heirloom silver. And with three little ones around now, it might just be casual chaos. I won't be surprised if no one notices my new tablecloth, at least not right away. But maybe through the years its simple beauty will become a part of our Thanksgiving Day celebration, like the food, the dishes, and the conversation. And maybe many years from now one of my grandchildren will pull my crewel work tablecloth from a drawer and remember the warmth of Thanksgiving Day at Gramma and Papa's house.

Mary Skarmeas lives in Danvers, Massachusetts, and has recently earned her bachelor's degree in English at Suffolk University. Mother of four and grandmother of three, Mary loves all crafts, especially knitting.

Grace

Dana Kneeland Akers

Great Spirit, bless this house and bless
The bread we break in thankfulness.

Keep firm the bonds that bind each heart,
Each to its own, though leagues apart.

Grant us the willingness to share
With those less fortunate to care

That there are multitudes whose woe
Is greater than is ours to know.

Great Spirit, guard and guide, we pray;
And may we not forget to say

With each day finished or begun,
"Thy will, Thy will alone, be done!"

Create within us, our Father, that true gratitude that shall make this day of Thanksgiving one of rededication, when we shall think not of how much we can eat but of how thankful we ought to be.

—*Peter Marshall*

Remember When

BUCKWHEAT PANCAKES

Edna Jaques

I wonder if people still eat buckwheat pancakes, the old-fashioned kind that you start in the fall in a heavy crock and keep going all winter. Do they still make them in country kitchens, the air blue with smoke and grease, and little blobs of slopped-over batter burning on the stove?

My mother used to start them, not too early in the fall, just when mornings began to get real cold. We'd be getting along fine on fried potatoes and pork or porridge, toast, and syrup, and then one day Dad would begin, "Say, when are we going to start the buckwheat pancakes?" and suddenly everyone in the house would get hungry for them as if they had been hungry all the time and didn't know what ailed them.

Maw would hum a little tune (she always started new things by singing a tune.) She would dig up the old heavy brown pitcher she made them in and begin to stir up a batter: first a pinch of salt, then two cups of warm water and a yeast cake, two tablespoons of brown sugar (to help the yeast grow), a few handfuls of white flour, and four handfuls of buckwheat flour. That's the way she

measured everything, by the handful, and the pancakes were on their way.

She'd let them rise in a cool place—usually the windowsill of the pantry—until the next night, when the mixture would be bubbling and alive. Then she'd add a few more cups of warm water (depending on the crowd she had to feed), a few more handfuls of white flour, and then enough coarse brown buckwheat flour to make a good batter that would pour easily. This was set in the pantry for the night, and by morning it was always running over the top and ready for the baking.

We had an old-fashioned griddle, half the size of the cookstove; this was allowed to get smoking hot and Dad would stand with a thick slice of salt pork on a fork and grease the griddle; then the batter was poured on in little precise rounds that baked quickly. A quick flip with the turner and the other side was browned to perfection, carried to your plate, and flopped down with a satisfied grunt from Dad;

I have
yet to taste
anything on earth
that can beat buckwheat pancakes
on a cold winter morning.

Of course, you had to have a good slice of fried salt pork to go with them, and syrup to sweeten the whole plateful. But you had something, a warm, filling meal that stayed with you for hours, whether you drove a load of wheat to town at forty below or went to the hills and cut wood, or just did chores.

When life crowds in on me and I am tired and worn and busy, I sit and think about the old breakfasts we used to have at home; I am heartened and comforted by the remembrance of a pile of buckwheat pancakes, swimming in syrup with a good slice of salt pork on the side of the plate waiting for me.

Homecoming

Evelynn Merilatt Boal

Ah, coming home
    Is always ever best,
No matter where I've been
    Or what I've seen.
It's here, at my own hearth,
    My mind can rest;
Before this fire,
    My soul becomes serene.
I do not mind
    A shabby chair or two.
It's comfort counts in this,
    My private place.
I can relax,
    Enjoy the things I do,
And wear my
    "This-is-how-I'm-feeling" face.
On walls and shelves,
    In every little nook
Are pictures and reminders
    Of good friends.
A quilted star,
    A figurine, a book—
Each treasured piece
    Its rare nostalgia lends.
Attachments call to places
    Far and near—
But none surpass
    The sweet "belonging" here.

NEW ENGLAND FARMHOUSE
Meredith, New Hampshire
William Johnson/Johnson's Photography

CORNER

NAPKIN RINGS

by Andrea Zywicki

COLLECTOR'S

As a little girl, I remember with tenderness the times our extended family gathered together to celebrate holidays, graduations, and weddings at the home of my favorite aunt, Christine. I was always eager to visit with relatives I didn't see often. As the women of our family bustled around the kitchen, my aunt would climb to the top cabinet to retrieve her best china and linens. On such occasions, she always gave me the honor of setting the holiday table. My favorite part was opening a red velvet-lined box that held my aunt's treasured silver napkin rings; engraved with violets, they had ruffled edges that reminded me of lace. I was careful with each piece as if it were the rarest gem, and I would delight in folding the linen napkins just right before tucking them in the rings. Once the table was set, the napkin rings captured my attention throughout the meal.

Remembering my love for her napkin rings, Aunt Christine gave me my own silver-plated set on my sixteenth birthday. Atop each piece is a small silver kitten playfully chasing a ball of yarn around the ring. The kitten has dark green eyes made of glass, and engraved lines mark his fur and the strands of yarn on the ball. The unique pieces became the first and favorite in my own napkin ring collection.

Always on the lookout for the next unusual napkin ring, I scour antique shows, auctions, and yard sales for new additions to what has become a grand collection that includes rings made of everything from china, silver, and glass to wood, ivory, and celluloid. My best find was a silver, Victorian napkin ring that I discovered at an estate sale on a country road near my home. After polishing it well, I could read the manufacturer's markings and realized that the ring was made by the Middletown Plate Company, well-known for its silver-plated, Victorian pieces. The piece is actually part of a combination set that features not only a diamond-shaped napkin ring, but a butter plate and salt and pepper shakers shaped like two bonneted girls. Such figural pieces (shaped like humans, animals, or objects) can be quite expensive, but I was able to take the set home for a small portion of its worth.

Figural rings such as this are usually either silver or silver plated, which does make them somewhat more expensive. Nevertheless, I have quite a few in my growing collection of napkin rings, with shapes ranging from cherubs to soldiers to chairs, each with intricate, carved detail.

As I look at the glass curio cabinet that holds my napkin ring collection, I think of the stories each napkin ring tells about a part of my life. Some remind me of places I've been, others of special people I've known. The silver kitten rings represent my relationship with my dear aunt, and others are reminders of Saturday afternoon shopping trips. One ring with the word *Colorado* painted across it is a memory of a family vacation, and a carved wooden ring symbolizes an old friendship.

When I was a young girl, special days with family always called for Aunt Christine's exquisite napkin rings. Although I cherish each of the dozens of napkin rings in my collection, I put them to good use as often as possible. Now that I have my own family and my own napkin rings, I like to make every day together a special occasion and an opportunity to add even more memories to my collection.

A Ring of Truth

If you would like to start a collection of napkin rings, here are some interesting facts:

History

•Napkin rings came into use in the seventeenth century after forks became popular with the upper class.

•The first napkin rings were made of silver, enamel, pottery, or glass.

•Victorians' napkins were kept as clean as possible and were washed only once a week. Napkin rings were used to identify each person's napkin.

•Napkin holders were first patented in 1867.

•In the middle of the nineteenth century, napkin rings were common in American, middle-class households and were most often made of ivory or bone.

•Figural napkin rings were first mass produced in 1869 through the use of electroplating. This helped make them affordable to Americans because until then only sterling silver figural napkin rings were available.

•American Victorian figural napkin rings are all silver-plated, whereas most sterling ones are British.

•Figural napkin rings lost popularity during the austere period caused by World War II, and it wasn't until the 1950s that they were popular again.

Focusing Your Collection

Due to the wide variety of napkin rings, many collectors narrow their searches to one category. For example:

•Napkin rings made in a particular decade, period, or region.

•Figurals featuring certain characters such as birds, Huckleberry Finn, fruit, or Kate Greenway children.

•Napkin rings made out of materials such as wood, glass, china, or celluloid.

•Travel-related napkin rings from particular cities, countries, or sites.

ANTIQUE SILVER NAPKIN RINGS. Jessie Walker Associates.

What to Look For

Being informed about the facts of napkin ring collecting can help you find a good buy. Here is some information that will help you determine the value of a piece:

•Any chips or scratches on a piece greatly depreciate its value.

•Purchasing a guidebook that includes pictures of valuable napkin rings as well as a list of silver-plate manufacturers will help you identify when pieces were made and by which manufacturer.

•Manufacturers' marks can be forged. Referring to a guidebook will help keep you from investing in a fake.

•Sometimes silver replating is used to hide reproductions.

•Figural napkin rings with parts attached by bolts are not necessarily fake. Some were made this way for easier cleaning.

•Suspicion should be aroused to figurals with bases that seem too large for the parts. The piece could have once been part of a combination set.

Autumn

Norma Fincher Hardwicke

Autumn's strutting by again,
Showing off her newest frills,
Throwing orange and yellow shawls
Across the valleys, trees, and hills.

Ridiculing Summer's lace,
She tosses auburn locks aside
And trims her shirt with sturdy fringe
Of golden acorns worn with pride.

Modeling her tartan skirt
Of flaming sumac-red and tan,
She skips through throngs of whispering leaves,
Painting them with artist's hands.

Adorned with Fall's coronation jewels
Of amber, topaz, ruby, gold,
She frolics gayly through November,
Unafraid of Winter's cold.

Child's Grace

Frances Frost

I give thanks for the lovely-colored year,
For the marigold sun and slanting silver rain,
For feathery snow across the hemlock hills,
For the sailing moon twelve times grown full again.

I give thanks for my family—Father, Mother,
And all the happy things we do together;
For understanding, laughter, and for love,
Strong and warm in any kind of weather.

I Thank Thee

Caroline Eyring Miner

I thank Thee, Lord, for little things:
The kettle on the stove that sings;
A baby's cry; the dimpling pool
Where raindrops splatter; and the cool,
Dark shadows when the day is bright;
The stars that prick the cloak of night
And pin the sky so it won't fall;
The wondering eyes of children; all
The little seeds that lift the sod
And tell the secret that is God.

The Mist and All

Dixie Willson

I like the fall,
    The mist and all.
I like the night owl's
    Lonely call—
And wailing sound

    Of wind around.

I like the gray
    November day,
And bare, dead boughs
    That coldly sway
Against my pane.

    I like the rain.

I like to sit
    And laugh at it—
And tend
    My cozy fire a bit.
I like the fall—

    The mist and all.

Indian Summer

Alice M. Barber

There was leaf smoke in the valley
    And a tapestry of leaves
In muted autumn colors.
    And the stubble where the sheaves
Of grain awoke the memories
    Of summer's harvest gain
Was all tarnished gold with shadows
    From the sunshine and the rain.
Purple asters lined the fencerows,
    And the bittersweet glowed warm
Against the gray, stone border
    That divided farm from farm.
Hushed and warm, November lingered,
    Cast her magic over all,
Sadly, sweetly, with reluctance,
    Breathed a last good-bye to fall.

DAIRY FARM
Binghamton, New York
Superstock

Country CHRONICLE

Lansing Christman

A MORNING OF THANKSGIVING

When I awoke the other morning, I faced a whole new world. The first heavy frost had transformed the countryside into a crystalline loveliness. It was a pure rich morning of reverent meditation, truly a morning of Thanksgiving.

When the sun peered over the eastern hills, it revealed a morning of dazzling beauty. Pastures and fields and roadsides were snow-white, and the roofs of the houses and barns and sheds shimmered. Frost had slipped millions of diamonds on the grass and weeds, and the night had looped strings of brilliant pearls around the neck of the hills.

The morning brought flocks of robins to the dooryard dogwood trees for a Thanksgiving treat. My yard was their dining room, and the dogwoods were the tables from which they dined. The trees were loaded with berries of scarlet and red, glistening in the sheen of the new day's sun.

It was Thanksgiving for me, too, for I was thankful to God for a natural environment that brings the birds to my door with their joyful songs and carols. Here they come to nest in season in the bushes and trees. Here they come in coldest winter to dine from the dooryard feeders.

The leaves on the dogwood have fallen; the berries are gone. But I still have the birds. I hear the liquid warbles of the bluebirds as they play house and inspect the snow-dusted bird boxes in which they reared their young last spring. I hear the sweet song of the chickadees. And down in the woods, the blue jays and crows are calling.

And listen! The versatile song of the mockingbird can be heard right here in the dooryard holly tree. It moves me to pause, to meditate, and to give devout thanks to God for the beauty and goodness of the natural world in which we live.

The author of two published books, Lansing Christman has been contributing to Ideals *for more than twenty years. Mr. Christman has also been published in several American, foreign, and braille anthologies. He lives in rural South Carolina.*

Late Autumn

Isla Paschal Richardson

Autumn has come again. The time each year
When yellow leaves are falling. Johnson grass
Has gone to seed, but let no farmer hear
Me praise its graceful sceptres where it crowds
The edges of the fences. And the skies
Are very, very blue, while soft white clouds
Pile high and billowy. Large butterflies
Flit hurriedly, uncertain where to go.
The royal colors of the iron weed
And goldenrod are fading. All aglow
Are sunsets. On the dogwood trees the seed
Are bright red clusters. It has come again—
The season that is whispering "Amen."

Chimney Smoke

Brian F. King

November's latter days are merry
With mistletoe and holly berry,
With jade and tangerine retreat
Of wintergreen and bittersweet,
With ruddy apples, peaceful shires
Where glows the ash of autumn's fires,
With lonely vales where chill winds sing
A song of wild geese on the wing,
With deep content of gentle folk
Whose dreams are wreathed in chimney smoke.

NOVEMBER DAWN
Tucker County, West Virginia
Jeff Gnass Photography

Readers' Forum

Snapshots from Our Ideals Readers

ABOVE: Bernie Leson of Espanola, Ontario, sent us this photograph of her youngest grandson Davis O'Connell, age three.

RIGHT: Anthony Muccio's baby beagle Jill teeters on top of Scott Anderson's giant pumpkin in St. Marys, Pennsylvania. This snapshot was sent to us by the boys' grandmother, Patricia Wickett.

BELOW: Laura and Edd Dykman of Ypsilanti, Michigan, share this picture of their great-grandson Alec Larson, who is helping his parents choose a pumpkin from the patch.

ABOVE: Peg Brimmer of Hartford, Connecticut, mailed us this photograph of her granddaughter Courtney Paige Brimmer, age three, making pigs in a blanket with a family friend, Kathy.

THANK YOU Bernie Leson, Patricia Wickett, Laura and Edd Dykman, and Peg Brimmer for sharing with *Ideals*. We hope to hear from other readers who would like to share snapshots with the *Ideals* family. Please include a self-addressed, stamped envelope if you would like the photos returned. Keep your original photographs for safekeeping and send duplicate photos along with your name, address, and telephone number to:

READERS' FORUM
IDEALS PUBLICATIONS INC.
P.O. BOX 305300
NASHVILLE, TENNESSEE
37230

ideals®

Publisher, Patricia A. Pingry
Editor, Lisa C. Ragan
Copy Editor, Michelle Prater Burke
Production Manager,
Tina Wells Davenport
Editorial Assistant, Tara E. Lynn
Editorial Intern, Andrea Zywicki
Contributing Editors,
Lansing Christman, Deana Deck,
Pamela Kennedy, Patrick McRae,
Mary Skarmeas, Nancy Skarmeas

ACKNOWLEDGMENTS
BUCKWHEAT PANCAKES from *UPHILL ALL THE WAY* by Edna Jaques, published in Canada by Thomas Allen & Son Limited. SWAN SONG from *NEW ENGLAND HERITAGE AND OTHER POEMS* by Rose Koralewsky, copyright © 1949 by Bruce Humphries Inc. Used by permission of Branden Publishing, Boston. LATE AUTUMN from *AGAINST ALL TIME* by Isla Paschal Richardson, copyright © 1957 by Bruce Humphries Inc. Used by permission of Branden Publishing, Boston. THE MIST AND ALL by Dixie Willson, from *CHILD LIFE MAGAZINE*, copyright © 1924, 1952 by Rand McNally & Company. Used by permission of Dana W. Briggs. Our sincere thanks to the following author whom we were unable to contact: Lucy Larcom for HYMN.

CHOOSE THE PERFECT GIFT FROM THESE BEAUTIFUL *ideals* BOOKS

**MOST BELOVED
BIBLE PASSAGES**
(160 pages, hardcover)
$19.95
Order 40776A

AMERICA CELEBRATES
(160 pages, hardcover)
$19.95
Order 40717A

**IDEALS 50TH ANNIVERSARY
COLLECTOR'S EDITION**
(80 pages, hardcover)
$9.95
Order 11261A

**GOD'S BEAUTIFUL
WORLD**
(160 pages, hardcover)
$19.95
Order 40520A

**IN THE FOOTSTEPS OF
THE MASTER**
(160 pages, hardcover)
$19.95
Order 40431A

**GREAT AMERICANS:
ELEANOR ROOSEVELT**
(80 pages, hardcover)
$10.95
Order 40792A

**GREAT AMERICANS:
HARRY S. TRUMAN**
(80 pages, hardcover)
$10.95
Order 40784A

VICTORY
(80 pages, hardcover)
$9.95
Order 40687A

**THE GIFT
OF FRIENDSHIP**
(160 pages, hardcover)
$19.95
Order 40709A

IDEALS FRIENDSHIP
(88 pages, softcover)
$5.95
Order 1144XA

NEW!

IDEALS CHRISTMAS
(88 pages, softcover)
$5.95
Order 11466A
5-PACK OF
IDEALS CHRISTMAS
(Includes free
gift envelopes)
$20.95
Order 52243A

**PRAYERS AND POEMS
FOR CHRISTMAS**
(160 pages, hardcover)
$19.95
Order 40741A

HE TOUCHED THEM
(160 pages, hardcover)
$19.95
Order 40830A

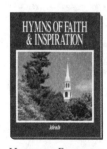

**HYMNS OF FAITH AND
INSPIRATION**
(160 pages, hardcover)
$19.95
Order 40415A

**SLIPCASE HOLDS 1 FULL
YEAR OF IDEALS**
$9.95
Order 10796

JOLLY OLD SANTA CLAUS
(32 pages, hardcover)
$14.95
Order 40806A

NEW!

**THE NIGHT BEFORE
CHRISTMAS**
(32 pages, hardcover)
$10.95
Order 40849A

**THE NIGHT BEFORE
CHRISTMAS**
(24 pages,
heavy board)
$5.95
Order 4089XA

CHRISTMAS MEMORIES
(48 pages, hardcover)
$14.95
Order 85672A

If your order totals
$25 or more, you receive
A FREE GIFT!

FOR FURTHER INFORMATION OR TO ORDER BY CREDIT CARD, PLEASE CALL TOLL-FREE 1-800-558-4343.
For Christmas delivery, we must receive your order by December 4.
We're sorry, but we are unable to ship orders outside the United States.